GREAT AMERICAN

HORSES

AN IMAGINATION LIBRARY SERIES

PAINTS AND PINTOS

by Victor Gentle and Janet Perry

Gareth Stevens Publishing
MILWAUKEE

For a free color catalog describing Gareth Stevens' list of high-quality books and multimedia programs, call 1-800-542-2595 (USA) or 1-800-461-9120 (Canada). Gareth Stevens Publishing's Fax: (414) 225-0377. See our catalog, too, on the World Wide Web: gsinc.com

Library of Congress Cataloging-in-Publication Data

Gentle, Victor.
    Paints and pintos / by Victor Gentle and Janet Perry.
        p.   cm. — (Great American horses: an imagination library series)
    Includes bibliographical references (p. 23) and index.
    Summary: Describes the physical characteristics of both paint and pinto horses and what differentiates these two breeds.
    ISBN 0-8368-2132-7 (lib. bdg.)
    1. American paint horse—Juvenile literature.   2. Pinto horse—Juvenile literature.
[1. American paint horse.   2. Pinto horse.   3. Horses.]   I. Perry, Janet, 1960-   .
II. Title.   III. Series: Gentle, Victor.   Great American horses.
SF293.A47G45   1998
636.1'3—dc21   98-14791

First published in 1998 by
Gareth Stevens Publishing
1555 North RiverCenter Drive, Suite 201
Milwaukee, WI 53212 USA

Text: Victor Gentle and Janet Perry
Page layout: Victor Gentle, Janet Perry, and Renee M. Bach
Cover design: Renee M. Bach
Series editor: Patricia Lantier-Sampon
Editorial assistants: Mary Dykstra and Diane Laska

Photo credits: Cover, pp. 7, 9, 13, 15, 17, 19, 21, 22 © Bob Langrish; p. 5 © Bob Pool/Tom Stack and Associates; p. 11 © Photofest.

Printed in the United States of America

1 2 3 4 5 6 7 8 9 02 01 00 99 98

Front cover: Paints and Pintos cover a lot of ground when it comes to horse work. This one could be a **dressage** horse, a cow horse, or a movie star!

TABLE OF CONTENTS

Words that appear in the glossary are printed in **boldface** type the first time they occur in the text.

HAVE PATCHES, WILL TRAVEL

A few hundred years ago, invaders from Europe arrived in the Americas. They brought horses with them on their journey.

American Indians had never seen anything like these great, frightening beasts, but they quickly learned how valuable horses could be. By capturing or stealing them, American Indians created their own stock. Horses made it possible for them to follow buffalo herds, meet other people, find good farmland, and explore the surrounding area.

Many of the horses brought over by the invaders had patterns of white and black, or white and other colors. They were called Paints, or Pintos. American Indians prized these patterned horses.

Traveling patches. A mare and **foal** on the move. Patterned horses are called by many names, including Calico, Paint, Patch, Pinto, and Indian Pony.

RIDE SAFELY. WEAR YOUR PATCH!

Many American Indians painted their faces and bodies to camouflage and keep themselves safe in times of danger.

They believed Nature had "painted" horses with color patches to keep them safe from evil spirits. So, anyone who rode a painted horse would be protected, too.

Sometimes a painted horse has a "medicine hat" pattern. It looks like the horse is wearing a hat. American Indian shamans (who are like priests and doctors rolled into one) would have a hat for making medicine. So, a horse given a medicine hat by Nature had to be very special indeed.

This foal looks like he is wearing a medicine hat over his ears. He also has watch eyes — one blue eye and one brown eye.

DON'T JUDGE A HORSE BY ITS COVER

Paints and Pintos can have a variety of patches and patterns. The color patches may be **palomino** (yellow), chestnut (reddish brown), dark brown, dun (brownish yellow or bluish gray), or black.

The patches might be one of two patterns, or a mixture of both: tobiano or overo. If you poured a pail of white paint over a horse's back, the pattern of the splash would be tobiano. If the horse were upside down when you poured the paint, the pattern of the splash would be overo.

Paint and Pinto eyes may be both brown, both blue, one brown and one blue (called "watch eyes"), or very light blue (called "glass eyes").

Look closely. Can you tell if any of these horses is a tobiano or an overo?

STAR-QUALITY SPOTS

Unlike most movie stars, the horse named *Fritz* had Pinto coloring. He was small, but brave. He leaped through windows, swam in powerful river rapids, and jumped over fires. With a quick signal from his human costar, Fritz would play dead. And he always fought the bad guys.

William ("Bill") Hart, Fritz's cowboy costar, swore that Fritz once saved him from drowning. What a horse!

Bill felt Fritz was his friend. He said he would do a movie for free if the studio would give him Fritz. The studio agreed. Fritz cost Bill a lot of money. "But," said Bill, "he was worth it, and the old snoozer is worth it, still."

It looks like Bill and Fritz are tricking the bad guys again. Fritz "plays possum," while Bill waits for them to run out of "ammo."

PALS, INDEED

Fritz was a favorite of more than one generation of movie-goers — kids and their parents. But lots of animals besides Bill were Fritz's friends.

Fritz raised money to help animals that were hurt during World War II. During one parade, people filled his saddlebags with so much money, Bill could not keep count of it.

When Fritz could be with his closest friends — Cactus Kate, the mare, and Lisabeth, the mule — he worked especially hard. After Fritz retired, the three friends lived the rest of their lives together on Bill's farm.

Horses enjoy company because they are herd animals — they survive best in groups. Here, two Paint horses make friends with a "medicine hat" kitten.

PATCHES + HORSE = PINTO OR PAINT?

Until about twenty years ago, any patched horse could be called either a Pinto or a Paint. In fact, the Spanish word *pinto* means "painted." However, not all painted horses can be formally **registered** as Paints or Pintos.

A **breed** is a group of horses that has been carefully **bred** by people for certain features. When a horse is bred, a person selects a mare (a female horse) and a stallion (a male horse) to mate and produce foals (baby horses). Hopefully, the foals will have their parents' features. To be registered, a horse's **conformation** must meet certain standards.

A handsome Tennessee Walking Horse Pinto. The rules say it cannot be called a Paint because its parents were not registered Paints, Quarter Horses, or Thoroughbreds.

PAINTS AND PINTOS: THE SAME, BUT DIFFERENT

In Fritz's movie days, he was called a Pinto. Today, he would be called a Mustang. Not all horses with Fritz's coloring can be registered as Paints and Pintos.

Paints are registered under different rules than Pintos. A Paint must have parents that are registered Paints, Thoroughbreds, or Quarter Horses. A Pinto may have parents that are almost any registered breed.

Both Paints and Pintos must have a patch of either color or white on their hides. They also have to be at least 14 **hands** high (about 4 feet 8 inches, or 1.4 meters, tall) at the **withers**.

16

The fighting stallion with the overo pattern and two colors in its mane may look like a Paint or a Pinto. However, according to the rules, it is a Mustang.

PAINT JOBS

When new settlers started ranches and farms in the American West one to two hundred years ago, they captured Mustangs. Mustangs were mostly Spanish horses that had strayed and were left to roam the plains. Many of these were beautiful painted horses.

That is why the Spanish word *pinto* was given to their coloring. Because the horses were wild, the American ranchers got them for free.

Looking at their strikingly varied coats, it is easy to imagine Pintos or Paints working as movie stars in westerns, like Fritz.

A Pinto at work, driving cattle. A predator might miss a Pinto on these snowcapped hills, since the horse's spots work as a natural camouflage.

EVERYDAY PATCH JOBS

Other Pintos and Paints may not be as famous as Fritz, but they are stars of their own shows.

Fritz was representative of the kinds of Western horses that work on ranches. They work as cutting horses, which are horses that chase calves from herds of cattle. They also work in rodeos and sometimes compete in barrel racing. Some are seen in English riding events, such as jumping and cross-country racing.

Paints and Pintos can be easily identified by their spots and patches. But, the types of jobs they do can be as different as the colors and patterns that splash across their backs.

Matching manes! This American Indian and her painted Paint horse present an eyeful of color!

DIAGRAM AND SCALE OF A HORSE

Here's how to measure a horse with a show of hands.
This red overo Paint has at least one blue eye and
a "bald" face that is mostly white.

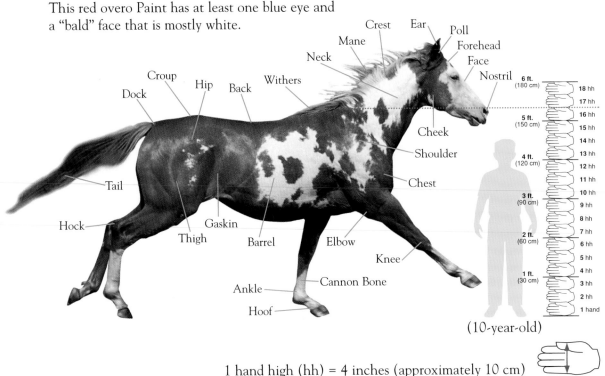

(10-year-old)

1 hand high (hh) = 4 inches (approximately 10 cm)

WHERE TO WRITE OR CALL FOR MORE INFORMATION

American Paint Horse Association
2800 Meacham Boulevard
Fort Worth, TX 76167
Phone: (817) 834-APHA (2742)

MORE TO READ AND VIEW

Books (Nonfiction):   *After Columbus: The Horse's Return to America.* Viola J. Herman
(Soundprints)

The Complete Guides to Horses and Ponies (series). Jackie Budd
(Gareth Stevens)

A Day in the Life of a Horse Trainer. Charlotte M. Freeman (Troll)

Great American Horses (series). Victor Gentle and Janet Perry
(Gareth Stevens)

Horses. Animal Families (series). Hans Dossenbach (Gareth Stevens)

Magnificent Horses of the World (series). Tomáš Míček and
Dr. Hans-Jörg Schrenk (Gareth Stevens)

Wild Horse Magic for Kids. Animal Magic (series). Mark Henckel
(Gareth Stevens)

Books (Fiction):   *Medicine Hat Horse.* Marguerite Henry (Rand McNally)

Patches. Lois Szymanski (Camelot)

Saddle Club (series). Bonnie Bryant (Gareth Stevens)

Videos (Fiction):   *The Black Stallion.* (MGM Home Video)

National Velvet. (MGM/UA)

WEB SITES

American Paint Horse Association:
www.apha.com

For interactive games:
www.haynet.net/kidstuff.html

For general horse information:
www.haynet.net
www.bcm.nt
okstate.edu/breeds/horses

Due to the dynamic nature of the Internet, some web sites stay current longer than others.
To find additional web sites, use a reliable search engine with one or more of the following
keywords to help you locate information about horses: *equitation, Mustangs, Quarter Horses,
racing, Tennessee Walking Horses,* and *Thoroughbreds.*

GLOSSARY

You can find these words on the pages listed. Reading a word in a sentence helps you understand it even better.

breed (n) — a group of horses that share the same features as a result of the careful selection of stallions and mares to produce foals 14, 16

breed (v), **bred** — to choose a stallion and a mare with certain features to produce foals with similar features 14

conformation (CON-for-MA-shun) — the way a horse's body is built 14

dressage (druh-SAHJ) — the performance, by a horse, of very precise movements at signals from its rider 2

foals (FOHLZ) — baby horses 4, 6, 14

hand — a unit used to measure horses equal to 4 inches (10.2 cm), about the width of the human hand 16, 22

palomino (PAL-oh-MEE-no) — a color of horse, one with a gold body and a white mane and tail. Palomino coloring can occur in many horse and pony breeds 8

registered — conforming to certain rules set by a group of breeders, and formally listed as belonging to that breed 14, 16

withers (WITH-erz) — the ridge between the shoulder bones of a horse. A horse's height is measured to its withers 16, 22

INDEX